THE
Secrets Tree

a novel by
June Counsel

illustrated by
Anthony Morris

D1439901

*I*ntroduction

Em's dad had to go into hospital ...

*... so Em was sent to stay with
her Aunt Deb in the country.*

Em really missed her dad, her home in London and all her friends.

Aunt Deb never seemed to have time for her.

Poor Em felt very cross and lonely, until one day, one surprising day...

CHAPTER ONE

"There," said Aunt Deb, "now you've got everything."

She handed Em a hand-drawn map. "Keep to the paths," she said. "Don't wander off. If you *do* get lost, blow your whistle and give a shout, there are Foresters about. Off you go and find the Wild Service Tree and have a lovely afternoon!"

Em strode off, scowling. I will *not* have a lovely afternoon, she thought grimly. To begin with it's freezing, and I'm not *interested*. I might be interested if I had a friend with me.

The village school came into Em's mind. She'd only been there a fortnight. Gary and Jim were fun, but – she *knew* they didn't like her.

"Wild Service Tree," she muttered. "Don't think I'm going to like you just because Aunt Deb does. I bet you're the dullest tree ever."

Em reached the entrance to Telling Wood, and shivered. It was scary; like entering another world, an old, old world, ruled by trees. It was winter and the branches were bare. Only the hollies were bright with leaves and berries.

Em pulled out Aunt Deb's map and studied it. "Down this path, turn left, then right ... oh, I see." She set off confidently.

Em walked and walked, but never came to the Wild Service Tree! Finally, she stopped, and said furiously, "Where *is* this tree, then?"

A man appeared as if by magic. He had a jay's blue feather in his hat and a badge on his jacket.

"Can I help? Let me introduce myself. I'm Dave Howitt, Forester, and I look after Telling Wood."

Em stabbed her finger at the picture of the Wild Service Tree in Aunt Deb's little *Pocket Book of Trees*. "I'm trying to find this *stupid* tree that my Aunt Deb thinks is so wonderful!"

"Hey, no tree's stupid! And you're nearly there. Up that slope to the top and it's there. May I have a look at your book, please?"

He held out his hand and Em gave him the book. He turned the pages gently until he came to the blank page at the front. On it was written, "From D to D with love."

"Are you staying with Miss Birch, then?" Dave asked.

"Yes," Em answered. "She's my aunt. I'm staying with her while my dad's in hospital."

Dave pulled a printed map from his pocket. "Well, have this. It's a little clearer than your aunt's map." He gave her back the book. "Enjoy the tree."

He walked off and Em started up the slope. Suddenly she felt much happier, almost looking forward to seeing the Wild Service Tree.

But when she did see it, when she *did* –

"*Enjoy?*" she shouted at it. "Enjoy *you?*" And she stared up at it, hands on hips, in disgust.

For it wasn't at all interesting. It had a few reddish-brown berries hanging from it, a few papery brown leaves, rather like little hands. Rage welled up in Em. She searched for a sharp stone to cut YOU ARE BORING in its bark, then stopped. Dave wouldn't like that.

"It's not your fault," she told the tree. "*Everything's* boring round here."

A curious movement rippled across the tree. It's smiling, said Em's imagination quickly. Then the tree pointed.

Em stared. It *did*. The tree pointed. She felt odd. This was – was – "I'm not going to use the word *magic*," she said, using it.

The tree was still. You saw me, it seemed to say. I'm not doing it again. Use what you saw.

"All right then," Em said. "You want me to go that way, I'll go that way."

She stomped along for a few yards and saw a splendid tree a little way ahead. It had a great broad trunk, huge roots that stuck up out of the ground and magnificent branches. "Now *you*," she said to it, "are something like a tree." Em sat down between two of the roots and emptied her pockets of all the things Aunt Deb had made her take. Two dry sandwiches, a bruised apple, an old orange, a sketchpad and a box of charcoal sticks.

"Because," Aunt Deb had said, "charcoal's perfect for sketching."

"But I'm not sketching," remarked Em, eating the sandwiches, "of all the boring things to do."

But the smooth white paper was inviting.
She picked up a pencil and wrote:

She drew a picture of herself being sick.
Then she folded the paper and pushed it
behind a piece of bark that was coming away
from the trunk.

"There, that's a secret," she told the tree.
"You keep it for me, and be my Secrets Tree."

Em picked up the things and stuffed them back in her pockets, but the apple and the orange she rolled into the bushes that grew under the trees. "For your friends," she explained to the tree. "I feel better now. You don't *know* how awful Aunt Deb's cooking is. She's a scientist, always writing papers. She lets things burn or not cook through, or else she just forgets to cook at all!"

"You do it then," said the tree.

"Me?" Em jumped. She stared at the tree. It didn't speak again, but its words were in her head, clear as clear. It was an old voice, but still strong and – it made Em feel very uncomfortable.

I'm getting out of here, she thought. She opened Dave's map and walked home as though ghosts were chasing her.

But she didn't go straight home. As she
walked up the village street thinking about
the awful meal that Aunt Deb would probably
throw together later on, she saw that the
village shop had mushrooms laid out on the
bench outside, big as dinner plates.

With the tree's words still sounding in her
head, Em went in. Big, comfortable Lottie
was behind the counter.

"How do you cook mushrooms?" Em
asked.

"Fry them," Lottie answered, and told
Em exactly how.

Em rushed home excitedly. She loved doing things. (It was only things Aunt Deb wanted her to do that she didn't like.)

"I'll cook supper tonight," she called, when she got in. "I won't drop or burn anything."

She hunted around and found a few potatoes and a forgotten egg at the back of the fridge. She made mashed potatoes with a little warm milk *and*, her own idea, a beaten-up egg. Then she fried the mushrooms to go with them.

"I didn't know you could cook!" cried Aunt Deb. "This is delicious."

"I didn't know either," smiled Em.

"That's the first time you've smiled since you came," laughed Aunt Deb. "You're much better-looking when you smile."

CHAPTER TWO

After this successful meal, Em took on most of
the cooking, and some of the shopping.

"I thought it would be boring, but it's
fun," she told Lottie.

"Food *is* fun," said Lottie, "and aren't we lucky to have it? Now, you go and smile at Ed next door and buy some of his famous sausages. Try making toad-in-the-hole with fried onion and a little chopped sage sprinkled in the batter. I'll come round and show you, if your aunt won't mind."

Aunt Deb did not mind. "Do," she said. "Show me, too. I could never make batter."

So Lottie came round and Em learnt how to make batter. I like feeding people, Em thought, because when I cook something for Aunt Deb and she says, "Oh, Em, that was good!" that makes *me* feel good. It's like us giving each other a present.

Aunt Deb had an old cat which Em hated. It left hair everywhere, was finicky about food and made disgusting noises when it washed itself.

One morning the cat was sick. Aunt Deb was busy typing, and so Em cleaned up the mess. "Ugh," she shuddered.

When she'd finished, she washed her hands, grabbed a fresh apple and a satsuma and headed for Telling Wood.

The minute Em was inside the wood, she felt better. As she passed it, the Wild Service Tree did its sideways ripple, only more so. It's laughing, said Em's imagination. "Trees don't laugh," Em said quickly, "it's the wind." But there was no wind. The day was perfectly still.

She walked on to the Secrets Tree and sat down between two comfortable roots. She ate her lunch, throwing the apple core into the undergrowth. "For your friends," she told the tree. Then she pulled out the sketch-pad and wrote:

I hate old cats
They SMELL
and SPEW
Old old cats
give me the
GRUE!

She drew a disgusting picture of the cat and stuck it down a crack in the bark.

"*I'm* old, " said the tree. "It's a privilege to be old." And it dropped one of its branches *almost* on top of Em!

"That could have killed me!" cried Em, jumping. "Then I'd never get old!"

She saw Dave the Forester coming towards her. "Look at that!" she cried, pointing at the fallen branch.

"Trees do that," Dave said. "They shed their branches as they get old, to give themselves less work. How is your aunt?"

"Busy," replied Em, "always typing."

"Yes," sighed Dave, "she always was."

Em walked back to the village thinking, I want to live to be old, but *nice* old, not cranky and smelly and sick. But – if people are too busy to notice and I'm too stiff and blind to hunt, I mean to shop ... well.

The fish van was driving slowly through the village. Em waved to it to stop, and asked the fishmonger, "What's a good fish for a finicky old cat?"

"For a fussy mog?" said the fishmonger. "Plaice is the thing." He sold her plaice for the cat, and some cod for herself and Aunt Deb, and told her how to cook both.

"Plaice!" screamed Aunt Deb when Em got home. "It's far too expensive!" But she didn't stop Em poaching it in milk for the cat, and she loved the fish pie Em made with the cod – topped with Em's famous mashed potatoes!

The cat loved the plaice. Afterwards Em groomed it with an old hairbrush. "I think it was hair balls making it sick," she said. The cat gave her a tiny lick as it settled down to sleep.

So life was better at Aunt Deb's, but not *much* better.

The village school was tiny and Em was not popular. There was always a crowd around Gary. There was always a group around Jim. But nobody went near Em.

The cracked grey bark of the Secrets Tree became quite stuffed with Em's hate notes.

I HATE not having anyone to talk to in break

I HATE SCIENCE
Aunt Deb explains
FOREVER!

I HATE living in the country MILES away from Putney and DAD

Writing out her hates was a relief, but – hating was beginning to be boring!

One dismal damp afternoon in Telling Wood she wrote:

I HATE MYSELF

... and didn't even bother to draw a picture.

"Try liking someone," said the tree.

"There isn't anyone *to* like," said Em. "They're *all* boring."

"Look around," said the tree.

Rain began to patter down. Em got to her feet. "*Around,*" repeated the tree.

Em walked round its massive trunk to where there was a split and a hollow space within. The rain beat faster. She dropped to her knees and squeezed inside.

"*Oh!*" she cried.

Pushed into cracks, hidden under leaves, were tiny squares of thin blue paper folded and folded and folded again.

Opened, they all said:

Wish tree, wish tree
Send me a friend.

A special, special friend
for me, me ME.

CHAPTER THREE

Bursting with excitement, Em crawled out of the Secrets Tree and raced back through the wood.

She ran straight into Dave, striding through the trees with an axe over his shoulder.

"Hullo, Em! Never seen you smile before! You look like a tree in spring. What's happened?"

"I found this in the Secrets Tree!" cried Em, showing him one of the tiny blue notes.

"And which tree is that?" asked Dave, looking puzzled.

"The big hollow ash tree," said Em, who'd looked it up in Aunt Deb's book. "I'm going to come every day till I find who wrote this."

"You do that," said Dave warmly. "If it's Red Riding Hood, we'll make her welcome. If it's the wolf, I'll come running with my axe."

When Em got home, she found Aunt Deb by the telephone looking pink and – and – different! Her voice was wobbly.

"D-Dave's just rung, Em. I-I mean Mr Howitt, the Forester, whom you met. He says you're planning to go up to your Secrets Tree in Telling Wood every day, to try to meet someone. Is that true?"

Em thought, Dave knows, Aunt Deb knows, so the Secrets Tree isn't a secret any longer. She felt sad, as though she'd lost something. But perhaps, she thought, there's always a time for a secret to be told. "Yes, I am," she said to Aunt Deb. "I'm going to go again and again and again till I find out who wrote this."

And out came the tiny blue note again.

Again and again and again Em went, but
always the hollow space was empty. There
were no new notes and the old ones grew
soggy and dirty, but Em didn't give up.

"You're a trier," said the tree, and it
sounded pleased.

A day came when it rained so hard, it seemed the world was made of water.

"You *can't* go to Telling Wood in this," cried Aunt Deb.

"I can," said Em, and she went.

Squelch, squelch, squelch!

The mud was so thick it tried to pull her wellies off and every brook was brimming.

The Wild Service Tree didn't mind. It did
its sideways ripple so strongly it was like a
laugh. It's cheering me on, thought Em. She
came breathlessly up to the Secrets Tree and
leaned against it, panting.

How soggy my hate notes will be, she
thought. Then she heard another watery
sound. Someone crying.

Stumbling round, kneeling down, peering into the hollow space, she said, "Don't cry. I'm Em. I've found you."

She crawled in. In the dim light she saw a small Chinese face, smudged with tears, and felt an ice-cold hand still holding a pen.

"I'm Em,' she said again. "I'll be your friend."

There was a gasp, then a watery giggle and the Chinese girl said, "Oh, *please!* I'm Jackie."

They crawled out of the hollow and stood up. The rain was crashing down.

The first brook they came to had turned into a torrent and Jackie, who was small, sank over her wellies in the foaming water.

"Wait," commanded Em, hauling her out. "Just stand there." She pulled her whistle out and blew three long blasts. And again. And again.

The rain hissed down, the wood darkened. Then they heard an answering whistle and soon Dave appeared.

"My goodness," he cried, "my word!" He took hold of their small chilled hands in his large warm ones. "Your aunt rang me," he said to Em. "She was worried sick about you." He scooped Jackie up in his arms and went striding off, with Em squelching joyfully beside him.

"Now then," he cried. "Into my Land Rover and I'll have you home in no time."

They bumped and splashed down the track to the village and up to Aunt Deb's cottage.

Aunt Deb went rather red as Dave came in, and stuttered and stammered, but still managed to make tea and toast for everyone.

When Jackie was dry and warm, Dave drove her home and Em went with them.

"Do you *know?*" she said when she got back. "Jackie's got an *enormous* family, but she's still lonely! All her brothers and sisters want to be accountants or lawyers, but Jackie just wants to dance!"

CHAPTER FOUR

From that day on, life was different for Em. Although Jackie went to another school, they met often; mostly by the Secrets Tree, sometimes in the little market town where Jackie's family had their take-away shop.

Having a friend made Em more friendly! Gary said to her one day, "You've changed, Em. You were *so* stuck-up, but now you're fun!"

"I was scared to speak to you," said Jim, "the scowl you had on your face!"

"I was homesick," Em explained. "My dad was rushed to hospital, so my gran shunted me down to Aunt Deb, who didn't want me!"

"Well, *we* do," Gary told her, "so forget about her."

Big, red-haired Jim was Lottie's son, and he *loved* to cook. Sometimes Em would go home with him and they'd both make supper for Lottie.

"I'm going to be a baker," Jim told Em. "Come into the kitchen and I'll show you how to make doughnuts."

Gary couldn't cook, but he could make
Em laugh more than anything on telly. He had
a rabbit called Bundle which liked to come
into the house. It would stretch out before the
fire between the dog and the cat, and stand no
nonsense from either of them.

But of all the new friends she made,
Jackie was the best. She was special. They
would go up to the Secrets Tree together,
taking picnic food, Chinese or English. They
would sit in the hollow space if it was wet, or
between the comfortable roots if it was dry,
and talk and talk and talk.

"I *wish* I could dance like you," Em would sigh. "But I'd fall over. I'm so clumsy."

"But you can draw!" Jackie would reply. "You draw so funnily, everybody laughs!"

Sometimes the boys came too, and then they didn't just talk, they walked, *miles!* Gary showed them where the badgers' sett was, and Jim took them to the foxes' earth.

CHAPTER FIVE

"We ought to write a thank-you letter to the tree," Jackie said one day. "And take it a present."

"A party!" exclaimed Em. "Yes! And invite Jim and Gary and the others."

So together they wrote out the invitations and Em drew a picture of the Secrets Tree with an invitation stuck in the bark.

Come to a party
at the SECRETS TREE
on Saturday
February 18th
at 4pm.

"Only," she said rather sadly, "it's not a Secrets Tree any longer, because I collected all my hate notes and burnt them, so it doesn't have any secrets now."

So the party preparations began. Em experimented with cake making. Her carrot cake was super. Her flapjacks were yummy, but her chocolate cake went funny and they ate it with spoons for pudding.

"Never mind," said Aunt Deb, licking her spoon. "It still tastes good. Try again. Experiments seldom work the first time."

Em wrote a last letter to the Secrets Tree.

Dear Secrets Tree,
Thankyou for listening to me. I must have bored you silly.
I don't hate any more. I love Jackie. I like Dave, Jim and Gary and Aunt Deb!! She's suddenly got nice.
Love Em
P.S. And the cat.

The night before the picnic a wind got up, and blew and blew and blew as though it would blow the world away.

In the morning the wind had gone and the world was still there, though very untidy.

Em packed up the picnic, Gary and Jim arrived with a bag of doughnuts and the three of them set off for Telling Wood. Jackie and the others were waiting at the entrance. Em led the way in, with Jackie close behind her.

The Wild Service Tree did not do its usual ripple as Em passed, but instead caught at her shoulder, then at her hair. "Don't," protested Em. "You're stopping me."

She rushed on ahead of the others, then stood still in shock.

The Secrets Tree was down, its great roots high in the air, wreckage all about it. Jackie's small hand crept into Em's.

"Come on, Em. We can still give it our thank-yous."

Together they stepped over broken branches to the fallen trunk and pushed their letters into its shattered bark. "No more secrets," mourned Em.

"One more," said the tree. "Mine!"

Startled, they looked about them, but saw only snapped twigs and torn-up earth. Then Em looked back up to the Wild Service Tree and saw it ripple and point. Yes, *point*.

"Oh!" Em cried. She went clambering over to where it pointed and found – a little metal box with "From D to D" engraved on the lid!

"Open it, open it," cried Jackie.

"No," said Em slowly, as two pictures flashed into her mind; Aunt Deb going pink as a winter sunset when Dave Howitt came in, and the words she'd seen written in the *Pocket Book of Trees*, "From D to D with love".

"It's not our secret, Jackie, but I think I know whose secret it is! I'll show it to Aunt Deb tonight, because – Dave's coming to supper!"

There was a shout from the others. "Come on, you two, the picnic's ready!"

So back they went and, sitting on the Secrets Tree's broad trunk, ate and drank and laughed and joked, until Em thought she had never, *never* been so happy.